Slavery in the United States
The "Abominable Trade"

Whitney Hopper

PowerKiDS press™

NEW YORK

Published in 2017 by The Rosen Publishing Group, Inc.
29 East 21st Street, New York, NY 10010

Copyright © 2017 by The Rosen Publishing Group, Inc.

Book Design: Samantha DeMartin

Photo Credits: Cover, DEA PICTURE LIBRARY/De Agostini Picture Library/Getty Images; p. 4, 11, 14, 18 Everett
Historical/Shutterstock.com; pp. 5, 6 DEA / G. DAGLI ORTI/De Agostini Picture Library/Getty Images; p. 7 courtesy
of Library of Congress; p. 8 Sipley/ClassicStock/ Archive Photos/Getty Images; p. 9 zeber/Shutterstock.com; p. 12
hutch photography/Shutterstock.com; p. 13 Florilegius/SSPL/Getty Images; p. 15 Hulton Archive/Getty Images;
p. 16 https://commons.wikimedia.org/wiki/File:The_Underground_Railroad_by_Charles_T._Webber,_1893.jpg;
p. 17 https://commons.wikimedia.org/wiki/File:Harriet_Tubman.jpg; p. 19 https://commons.wikimedia.org/wiki/
File:DredScott.jpg; p. 21 https://commons.wikimedia.org/wiki/File:Thure_de_Thulstrup_-_L._Prang_and_Co._-_
Battle_of_Gettysburg_-_Restoration_by_Adam_Cuerden.jpg.

Library of Congress Cataloging-in-Publication Data

Names: Hopper, Whitney, author.
Title: Slavery in the United States : the "abominable trade" / Whitney Hopper.
Description: New York : PowerKids Press, 2016. | Series: Spotlight on
  American history | Includes index.
Identifiers: LCCN 2015048099 | ISBN 9781508149538 (pbk.) | ISBN 9781508149408 (library bound) | ISBN
9781508149194 (6 pack)
Subjects: LCSH: Slavery--United States--History--Juvenile literature.
Classification: LCC E441 .H725 2016 | DDC 306.3/620973--dc23
LC record available at http://lccn.loc.gov/2015048099

Manufactured in the United States of America

CPSIA Compliance Information: Batch #BS16PK: For further information contact Rosen Publishing, New York, New York at 1-800-237-9932.

CONTENTS

SLAVERY IN AMERICA

Slavery has existed all over the world for thousands of years, from ancient Mesopotamia to Greece to England. However, it wasn't until 1619 that slaves were brought to the British colonies in North America.

The first slaves in the English North American colonies arrived on a Dutch ship called the *White Lion*. It held 20 African slaves captured from the Spanish. The Dutch traded these slaves to colonists in Jamestown, Virginia.

The first colony to legalize slavery was Massachusetts in 1641. Other colonies followed, especially as agriculture took hold in the New World.

As the population in the English colonies grew, the need for people to do farm work increased. At first, indentured servants did this work. Indentured servants were people who worked for someone in return for the cost of their passage to America. They were given a place to live and food to eat, and after a certain amount of years, they were free. Many indentured servants were from Germany, Ireland, or England, but some were African and they could become free blacks. After a while, however, the need for workers became too great. America turned to slavery.

A DEADLY JOURNEY

Slavery spread quickly after it became legal in English colonies. Slaves were brought over from Africa in crowded ships that held hundreds of people. The journey to America was risky for **immigrants**, but for slaves, it was a deadly crossing.

The journey from Africa to the Americas was called the Middle Passage. Former slave Olaudah Equiano wrote a book about his life, describing what it was like to make this deadly journey.

Many slaves came from west and central Africa. They were taken from their homes and sometimes traded by other Africans. They were forced to walk, chained to each other and without enough food, for hundreds of miles to the coast. Around 20 million Africans were stolen from their homes, but only half made it to the coast alive. Once there, slaves were kept in **dungeons** until a ship arrived.

Olaudah Equiano

Slave ships were known for their awful conditions. Hundreds of slaves were piled into the bottom of a boat. They were chained close together with little food, air, or room to move. Illness spread quickly, and it's believed that up to 20 percent of those transported on slave ships died there.

ARRIVING IN THE AMERICAS

The **transatlantic** slave trade was part of a triangular trade system between Europe, Africa, and the Americas. Slaves from west Africa were sent to the Americas to work on farms and plantations. The crops they raised were sent to Europe and to Africa to trade for more slaves.

Since many slaves were needed to tend to the sugarcane crop in the Caribbean and South America,

Slaves were bought and sold as property. They were valuable because of the work they could do, but they had no rights.

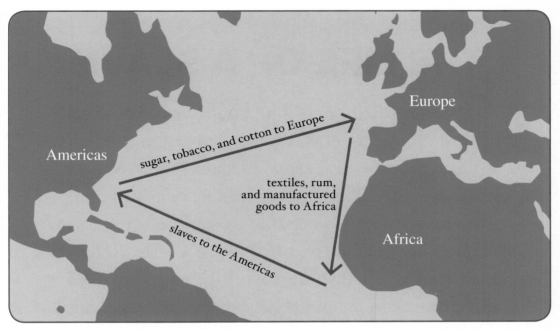

This diagram shows the triangular trade system that was responsible for widespread slavery in the Americas.

a majority of slaves were brought there in the 1600s and 1700s. Slaves in the Caribbean and South America were treated terribly. Many slaves died and they had few children, so more slaves had to be brought all the time.

African enslavement in the Americas increased greatly between 1720 and 1780. Conditions in the British colonies weren't much better than in the West Indies. However, slaves had more children in the colonies, so the population increased quickly. By 1860, one-third of the population in the southern United States was black and most of those were slaves.

THE LIFE OF A SLAVE

Slaves worked many long hours each day, usually from sunup to sundown. Some worked in the fields, and this was the hardest work of all. Overseers and drivers tried to get the most work out of the slaves. Some slaves were able to work as servants in the household, and their lives were a little better. Slave children had to start working as young as three or four years old. They were often small and sickly. By age 11, boys were working in the field.

There were many rules slaves had to live by. They couldn't learn to read or write. They had to be **obedient** to their owners. If a slave disobeyed or tried to run away, they could be killed. Because of this, slaves were completely dependent on their owners.

Slaves had little to no health care, so they often died young. They didn't have the right foods to keep them healthy and were always overworked. This led to many illnesses and injuries.

American slave women gave birth to an average of nine babies in their lifetime. They had to work right up until they gave birth, and they went back to work soon after.

THE RISE OF TOBACCO

America's first successful cash crop was tobacco. John Rolfe, who was a Jamestown colonist, brought a new kind of tobacco to the struggling colony. It grew well, and it was in high **demand** in England. Large farms called plantations began to pop up throughout the southern colonies. The greater the demand, the more workers were needed.

hanging tobacco

*Before tobacco, the colonial settlement in Jamestown, Virginia, was failing. After tobacco and slaves were brought to the British colonies, the **economy** boomed.*

Throughout the 1600s and 1700s, more slaves were brought from Africa to work on tobacco and rice plantations. Some farms were small and had only about five slaves. Some large plantations had over 100 slaves.

Slaves were often bought at public sales, which were called auctions. Owners would bring their slaves to auctions and try to get the best price for them. Although slaves often lived in houses as family groups, slave marriages were not seen as legal. Families were often broken up when members were sold to different owners.

THE COTTON BOOM

In the late 1700s, around the time America gained its independence, tobacco farming was starting to slow down. The South needed a new way to make money. The Industrial Revolution in Great Britain meant that cloth was easier to make, so cotton was in high demand.

Soon, cotton farms grew up throughout the South, with slaves picking and removing the seeds from each plant. The cotton industry boomed when Eli Whitney invented the cotton gin in 1793. This machine separated cotton and its seeds more easily. Production increased and more slaves were needed.

cotton gin

The issue of slavery became more of a dividing issue between the North and South as time went on. Many people in the North believed slavery should be abolished completely, while many of those in the South believed they needed slaves to survive.

As the South grew more dependent on slavery, the North began to see it as unnecessary. Unlike the South, the economy of the North didn't depend heavily on farming. All northern states had **abolished** slavery by 1804. Four years later, the United States made the transatlantic slave trade illegal. However, slave owners in the South continued to buy and sell slaves within the United States.

THE ABOLITIONIST MOVEMENT

Abolitionists were people who wanted to abolish slavery. They believed it was an "abominable," or awful, trade. They not only wanted slaves to be free, but also for **discrimination** to end. Abolitionists began to greatly increase in number in northern states beginning in the 1830s. The movement continued until around 1870, and it inspired social **activists** well into the 1900s.

The Underground Railroad was a network of hiding places created by abolitionists who helped runaway slaves escape to the North. They hid slaves and helped them run to different "stations" at night. Abolitionist and former slave Harriet Tubman helped more than 300 slaves escape.

One major cause of the growing abolitionist movement was a religious movement called the Second Great Awakening. It called for freedom for all people. Many famous abolitionists grew out of this movement. An abolitionist named William Lloyd Garrison began publishing a newspaper called the *Liberator* that supported freedom for all.

Another famous abolitionist was former slave Frederick Douglass, who was a talented writer and public speaker. Another abolitionist who used the power of words was Harriet Beecher Stowe, a white woman who wrote a novel called *Uncle Tom's Cabin*. This story of the horrors of slavery became one of the greatest American novels.

SLAVERY MOVES WEST

In the early to mid-1800s, America was growing. And with each state that was added, slavery could grow as well. In 1820, there was **tension** between free states and slave states over what would happen when new states were added. The result was the Missouri Compromise, which said that the new state of Maine would be free, while Missouri would have

Like the Missouri Compromise, the Compromise of 1850 was created to decrease tensions between the North and South on the issue of slavery. This picture shows senator Henry Clay introducing the Compromise of 1850, which dealt with the slave status of the states in the newly acquired Mexican Cession.

Dred Scott

legal slavery. It was also decided that any western U.S. land north of Missouri's southern border would be free.

In 1854, the Kansas-Nebraska Act made it possible for slavery to be legal in all new territories. This was based on popular sovereignty, or the idea that states could decide for themselves what they wanted.

Three years later, the Supreme Court ruled in the case *Dred Scott v. Sandford* that the federal government couldn't make slavery illegal in new states. It also said that African Americans couldn't be citizens even if they were free.

THE CIVIL WAR

In 1860 and 1861, southern states began seceding, or leaving, the United States. The 11 states that eventually seceded became the Confederate States of America. This sparked the American Civil War, which was fought from 1861 to 1865.

Abraham Lincoln was president during the American Civil War. His presidency was one of the big reasons why the southern states left the Union. Lincoln was against slavery, but he also wanted to unite the country. He wouldn't recognize the southern states as their own country, which led to the American Civil War. The first battle of the war was at Fort Sumter in Charleston, South Carolina, and the Confederates won. During the war, 140,500 freed slaves fought with the Union Army.

In 1863, Lincoln announced that all slaves in the southern states were free. His speech was called the Emancipation Proclamation. However, it would be years before southern slaves were truly free.

The Battle of Gettysburg in July 1863 was the major turning point in the war. Two years later, the South **surrendered** to the North, and the United States was united once again.

SLAVES AFTER SLAVERY

The 13th **Amendment** to the U.S. Constitution finally outlawed slavery for the whole country in 1865. However, former slaves in the South still faced great **poverty** and discrimination. Although they were full citizens under the 14th Amendment of 1868, they weren't treated equally.

Southern states passed laws and policies, known as Jim Crow laws, which took away African Americans' rights to go to court against whites or serve on juries. Other laws had to do with jobs and land ownership, while others set unfair punishments for small crimes. These laws were meant to keep free blacks from becoming successful or rising above their former slave status. In fact, many former slaves kept working for their former owners for little money because they had no choice.

It wasn't until the civil rights movement of the 1950s and 1960s that African Americans gained legal equality. Access to voting became easier for African Americans, and **segregation** in schools and public places became illegal. However, racism is still an issue in America today, stemming from centuries of slavery.

GLOSSARY

abolish (uh-BAH-lish): To officially end or stop something, especially slavery.

activist (AHK-tih-vihst): One who acts strongly in support of or against an issue.

amendment (uh-MEHND-muhnt): A change in the words or meaning of a law or document, such as a constitution.

demand (duh-MAND): A strong request for something.

discrimination (dihs-krih-muh-NAY-shun): Unfairly treating people unequally because of their race or beliefs.

dungeon (DUN-juhn): A dark, underground prison.

economy (ih-KAH-nuh-mee): The amount of buying and selling in a place.

immigrant (IH-muh-gruhnt): One who comes to a country to settle there.

obedient (oh-BEE-dee-uhnt): Willing to obey.

poverty (PAH-vuhr-tee): The state of being poor.

segregation (seh-gruh-GAY-shun): The forced separation of races or classes.

surrender (suh-REHN-duhr): To give up.

tension (TEHN-chun): A state of unrest or opposition between individuals or groups.

transatlantic (tranz-uht-LAN-tihk): Relating to crossing the Atlantic Ocean.

INDEX

PRIMARY SOURCE LIST

Cover: American Slave Market. Oil on canvas. Created by Taylor. 1852. Now kept at the Chicago History Museum, Chicago, IL.

Page 7: Detail from the frontispiece from *The Interesting Narrative of the Life of Olaudah Equiano, or Gustavus Vassa, the African.* Written by Olaudah Equiano, also known as Gustavus Vassa. Published in 1794 in London, England. Now kept at the Library of Congress, Prints and Photographs Division, Washington, D.C.

Page 17: Detail from the portrait of Harriet Tubman. Photograph. Created by H.B. Lindsley. Between ca. 1860 and 1875. Now kept at the Library of Congress Prints and Photographs Division, Washington, D.C.

WEBSITES

Due to the changing nature of Internet links, PowerKids Press has developed an online list of websites related to the subject of this book. This site is updated regularly. Please use this link to access the list: www.powerkidslinks.com/soah/slave